Unit

Let's Explore

Mc
Graw
Hill
Education

Contents

Pam can see a sap map.

Pam can see the .
path

Pam can see a .
man

Pam can see a  .
pail

Pam can see sap.

Pam Can See

Pam can see a  .
pot

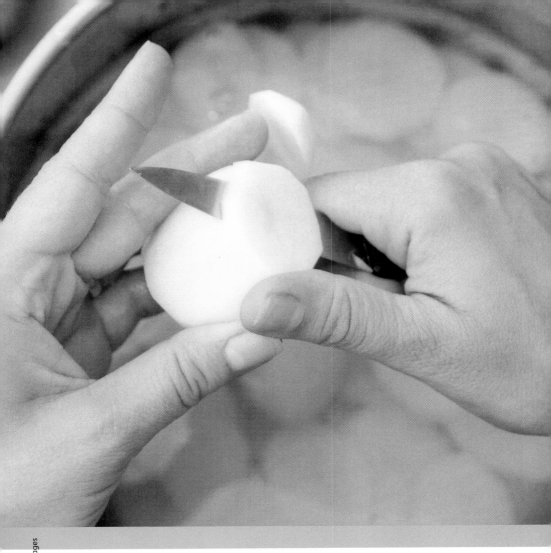

Pam can see a .

potato

Pam can see a .
cup

Pam can see the .

soup

Pam can see the  .

people

12

Tap the Mat

Sam can see a mat.

Sam can tap the mat.

Sam can tap the mat.

I like the mat Sam.

Tap the mat Sam.

I Am Pat

I sat at the  .
table

I can see the mat.

I like the 🍞.

toast

22

I like the ▰.

pie

23

Nicole S. Young/E+/Getty Images

I am Pat.

We See Tam

I am Tam.

I see Pam at the .

swing

I see Sam at the  .

table

I see a  .

cat

We like .

bugs

A Sap Map

DECODABLE WORDS
Target Phonics Elements
  Initial and Final Consonant *p*: map, Pam, sap

HIGH-FREQUENCY WORDS
a
Review: can, see, the

Pam Can See WORD COUNT: 23

DECODABLE WORDS
Target Phonics Elements
  Initial and Final Consonant *p*: Pam

HIGH-FREQUENCY WORDS
a
Review: can, see, the

Tap the Mat

DECODABLE WORDS
Target Phonics Elements
  Initial and Final Consonant *t*: mat, Sam, tap

HIGH-FREQUENCY WORDS
like
Review: a, can, I, see, the

I Am Pat WORD COUNT: 21

DECODABLE WORDS
Target Phonics Elements
  Initial and Final Consonant *t*: at, mat, Pat, sat

HIGH-FREQUENCY WORDS
like
Review: can, I, see, the

We See Tam

DECODABLE WORDS
Target Phonics Elements
  Review Letters *m, a, s, p, t*: am, at Pam, Pat, Sam, Tam

HIGH-FREQUENCY WORDS
a, like, see, the, we
Review: I

HIGH-FREQUENCY WORDS TAUGHT TO DATE
Grade K
a
can
I
like
see
the
we

DECODING SKILLS TAUGHT TO DATE

Initial and final consonant *m*; short *a*; initial *s*; initial and final consonant *p*; initial and final consonant *t*